HISTORIC
COMMUNITIES

A Colonial Town
Williamsburg

Bobbie Kalman

Crabtree Publishing Company

HISTORIC
COMMUNITIES

Created by Bobbie Kalman

For Isabelle Salvy

Editor-in-Chief
Bobbie Kalman

Research and editing
Jodi Gaspich

Illustrations and cover design
Antoinette "Cookie" DeBiasi

Cover art
John Mantha

Computer design
Antoinette "Cookie" DeBiasi

Color separations
ISCOA

Printer
Worzalla Publishing Company

Special thanks to:
Cathy Grosfils, Laura Arnette, John Caramia, Ken Kipps, Art Werner, Tiffany Martin, Samantha Crabtree, and Rebecca Jenney

Photographs:
Courtesy of the Colonial Williamsburg Foundation: cover, title page, pages 4 (top), 8 (top), 13 (top left), 13 (bottom), 14, 15, 16, 17 (center), 21, 22, 24, 28 (both), 29 (left)
Peter Crabtree and Bobbie Kalman: pages 4 (bottom), 5, 6, 7, 8 (bottom), 9 (both), 12, 13 (top right), 17 (bottom), 19, 20, 25, 26, 27, 28 (both), 31
Art Werner: page 30

Crabtree Publishing Company

350 Fifth Avenue	360 York Road, RR4	73 Lime Walk
Suite 3308	Niagara-on-the-Lake	Headington
New York, N.Y.	Ontario, Canada	Oxford 0X3 7AD
10118	LOS 1J0	United Kingdom

Cataloging in Publication Data
Kalman, Bobbie, 1947-
    A colonial town: Williamsburg

(Historic communities series)
Includes index.
ISBN 0-86505-489-4 (library bound) ISBN 0-86505-509-2 (pbk.)
This book looks at the lifestyles and customs of people who live in a colonial town, Williamsburg, Virginia.

1. Williamsburg (Va.) - Juvenile literature. I. Title. II. Series: Kalman, Bobbie, 1947-   . Historic communities series.
F234.W7K35 1992   j975.5'4252   LC 93-30204

Contents

Welcome to Williamsburg!

Each year thousands of people visit a town in the southeastern part of the United States, within the state of Virginia. It is called Williamsburg. The visitors come to walk through its quaint Historic Area and watch the tradespeople create handmade items in their shops. They listen attentively as costumed interpreters tell them how people lived and worked in the eighteenth century. Visiting Williamsburg is like stepping back in time.

A colonial town; an historic community

Nearly three hundred years ago, Williamsburg was a **colonial** town. It was built when Virginia was an English **colony**. A colony is a territory ruled by a faraway country. The people of Virginia, who were known as **colonists** or **colonials**, were considered English citizens even though they lived across the ocean from England. Williamsburg is called "an historic community" because it recreates a special time in history when Williamsburg was the capital city of Virginia.

Williamsburg is both a museum and a living city. Horsedrawn carriages "clippity-clop" through its Historic Area, where cars are not allowed to travel down the main road. Visit Colonial Williamsburg with us and learn how the city of long ago is still very much alive today.

Inside the fortified community, the settlers constructed a number of dwellings: a church, a storage house, and a guard post. The fort was named James Fort.

It all started at Jamestown

To understand the history of Colonial Williamsburg, let us travel back to the time and place where America began. Four hundred years ago, when North America was still a vast wilderness, a group of English explorers found Virginia and claimed it as an English colony. News about Virginia traveled quickly, and a group of Englishmen decided to settle in the New Land. On December 20, 1606, they left England in three ships: the Susan Constant, Godspeed, and Discovery. After four months of sailing through terrible storms, the settlers reached Virginia. They named the place where they landed "Jamestown," after James I, the King of England. Jamestown was the first permanent English settlement in America.

The tradesmen of Jamestown made furniture and tools for colonials.

James Fort

As soon as they arrived, the men began building a strong fort for protection. They chopped down trees and put up a high wall of logs around the new settlement. In spite of their hard work and determination, the settlers faced terrible times. Many died as a result of disease and starvation.

Eventually, however, the colonials learned how to survive in Virginia. In fact, many became wealthy from growing and selling tobacco. In the years that followed, more people came from England, and new settlements developed in other areas of Virginia. Although Jamestown was the capital of the colony, it did not grow larger because it was surrounded by low, swampy land.

The first settlers lived in small huts. Their beds were handmade from wood and rope. They slept on straw mattresses.

Williamsburg is born

In 1699 the statehouse of Jamestown, where representatives of the government met, burned down. The governor decided that the fire was a good reason to move the capital to a new place. That place was Middle Plantation. Middle Plantation was not swampy like Jamestown. It was located farther inland on dry, high ground.

Middle Plantation was a small community with only a few houses, a church, and a school. A path wound its way through the village. When the government moved into the area, hundreds of people came to live in the new capital. The new capital was named Williamsburg, in honor of William III, who was King of England at the time.

There were several inns and taverns in colonial Williamsburg because many people traveled there to conduct business or meet with government officials. When the courts were in session, the town was filled with visitors.

A bustling capital

A "palace" was built for the governor, and a statehouse was constructed as a meeting place for the members of government. Inns and taverns were built for the many visitors who came to the capital on government business. Shops were erected; homes were built. The new buildings were planned and constructed with great care. The land around the buildings came to life with blooming flowers, healing herbs, and neat garden hedges. Williamsburg was to become a special place because it was the capital of Virginia, and Virginia was the biggest English colony in North America.

A quiet town

For almost one hundred years, Williamsburg was an important center of politics and trade. Then, in 1780, the capital of Virginia was moved to Richmond. In the years that followed, the once-bustling city of Williamsburg became a quiet town and stayed that way for over a century.

The restoration of Williamsburg

Dr. W.A.R. Goodwin, who was the rector of Williamsburg's Bruton Parish Church in the 1920s, thought it was important to save Williamsburg's eighteenth-century buildings. He dreamed of restoring these buildings to look as they did in the past. He inspired John D. Rockefeller, Jr., to provide money for the project. Together, the two men made the dream a reality. Over the next thirty years, many of the original buildings of colonial Williamsburg were carefully restored. Today, Williamsburg is once again a bustling town. It is full of visitors who travel there to experience life in the past.

Many Williamsburg houses were symmetrical, or balanced, in appearance. For instance, the windows of the second floor of a house were placed directly above the windows of the first floor. The chimneys at either end of a house were the same height.

Behind the larger houses stood a number of outbuildings, including kitchens and smokehouses. There were also stables, barns, chicken coops, and outdoor toilets.

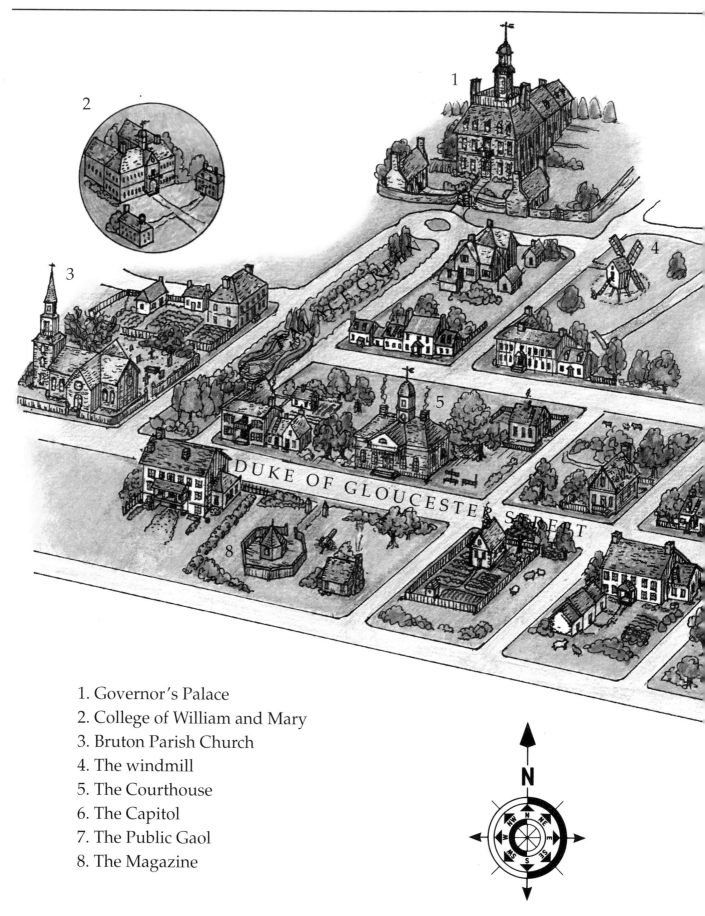

1. Governor's Palace
2. College of William and Mary
3. Bruton Parish Church
4. The windmill
5. The Courthouse
6. The Capitol
7. The Public Gaol
8. The Magazine

Map of Historic Area

This map shows many of the buildings in the
Historic Area of Colonial Williamsburg. The
inset picture is the College of William and Mary,
which is located two blocks west of Bruton Parish
Church. It is at the end of Duke of Gloucester
Street. Surrounding the Historic Area is the
modern city of Williamsburg.

7

6

Around town

(above) Shops and taverns with large colorful signs line busy Duke of Gloucester Street. (below) The view from behind the buildings is much different. Flowers, shrubs, herbs, and vegetables fill the backyards. It looks like a country scene.

There was no indoor plumbing in colonial days. People had to bring in water from outdoor wells.

Horses were very important to the colonials. They were used for transportation, and they helped perform many heavy jobs, such as planting crops and pulling loads.

Do you know why there is a ladder on the roof? It is for putting out chimney fires.

The governor was a wealthy and important man. He represented the king of England. Only very important people were invited to entertainments at the Governor's Palace.

The Governor's Palace

When the capital was moved from Jamestown to Williamsburg, a magnificent home was built for the governor of Virginia. The governor was appointed by the king to be his representative in Virginia. Only the governor could call a meeting of Virginia's lawmakers at the Capitol.

A grand estate

The Governor's Palace was the official residence of the governor. It displayed the power and authority of England, as well as the latest styles and fashions the governor brought from London. The gardens surrounding the estate were groomed by the governor's gardeners and were especially enjoyed by his guests. Within the walls of the palace complex were outbuildings such as a kitchen, stables, and servants' hall.

(above) The swords, pistols, and flags inside the Governor'sPalace reminded the colonists that the English army would defend Virginia against all enemies.

Public buildings

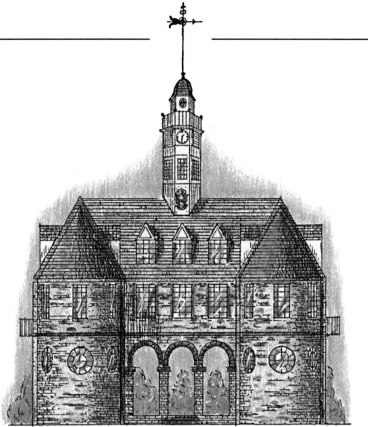

The Capitol was built in the shape of the letter "H." One side was for the House of Burgesses and the other for the Governor's Council. The section joining the two sides had the conference room where the two houses of government held their meetings. When the representatives from both bodies of government met, the event was called a General Assembly.

The Capitol

The lawmaking branch of government in Virginia was composed of two houses: the House of Burgesses and the Governor's Council. They met at the Capitol. The members of the House of Burgesses represented the colonists, and were elected by **property owners**. Only property owners who were free, white, Anglican men were allowed to vote in colonial Virginia. The Governor's Council consisted of twelve representatives appointed by the king. They represented the interests of the king. The Council also sat as judges in Virginia's General Court to make sure that laws were obeyed.

On the grounds of the Magazine, militiamen assembled for public affairs and to practice marching and firing their muskets and cannons. They needed to be prepared in case of war.

The Magazine

The Magazine served as a storage house for the cannons, guns, and ammunition that were used by Virginia soldiers. Free men between the ages of 18 and 55 were obliged to serve in the militia on **muster day** or on **slave patrol**.

The Courthouse

People who committed small offenses, such as petty theft, were tried at their local courthouse. The courthouse in Williamsburg served residents of James City County and the city of Williamsburg. Disputes over land boundaries, debts that were owed, and slave-ownership are examples of other typical courthouse trials. Judges, called **magistrates**, decided on the punishments for petty or minor lawbreakers.

The stocks and pillory

Those whom the magistrates found guilty of crimes could receive a public whipping or be placed in the **stocks** or **pillory**. The stocks held a person's ankles; the pillory forced prisoners to stand bent over with their heads and hands locked in a wooden structure. Both forms of punishment were extremely embarrassing. No one enjoys being ridiculed by others!

The Public Gaol

The Public Gaol, pronounced "jail," is Williamsburg's second-oldest brick structure. It was the place where people accused of serious crimes waited for their trials. The colony's two high courts each met twice a year, so the prisoners could be left in damp, dirty cells for several months before their cases were heard.

Cruel methods of punishment

In colonial times, very few people were given a prison sentence as a punishment. Prisoners who committed crimes such as horse theft, burglary, or murder were hanged. Other offenders were branded with a hot iron or had their ear cut off.

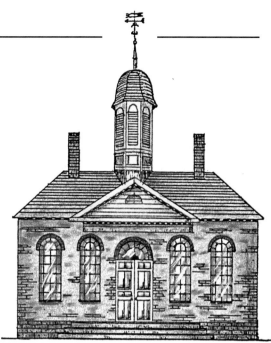

Two courts met at the Courthouse: the James City County Court and the city of Williamsburg Court. Each held trials once a month.

(above) A prisoner's neck and wrists were placed in the pillory, and he or she was forced to stand bent over for hours or days. (below) Some prisoners sat in the stocks instead. Both forms of punishment were meant to embarrass the offenders.

Bruton Parish Church

Bruton Parish Church was an Anglican church. The king of England was the head of both the Anglican church and the colony. The government and the church ruled the colony together. The church raised money by taxing the workers of the community. This tax was called a tithe.

The main church of old Williamsburg was Bruton Parish Church. Each week, citizens from all social classes gathered there for Sunday services. Church services were the only organized, formal setting in which all classes were together in one place. The rich landowners were seated at the front of the church near the pulpit and the servants at the back. The slaves were not allowed to sit with the other people. Everyone was required by law to attend church. Those who did not go at least once a month were fined or whipped!

The College of William and Mary

The College of William and Mary, named after the king and queen of England, was one of the few fine schools available in the colony. Boys between the ages of twelve and seventeen came from all over Virginia to attend the college.

Only boys from very wealthy families could afford to go to the school. Girls were not allowed to attend because people in those days did not think that women needed a formal education.

Learning to be gentlemen

At the college, young men learned the skills needed to become gentlemen. A gentleman was expected to be well-dressed, courteous, and well-spoken. He usually became a wealthy landowner or merchant.

The students who attended the college lived at the school. They wore long black robes during school hours. Their morning classes began at seven o'clock and lasted until eleven; the afternoon classes were from two to five o'clock. The students studied Greek and Latin as well as mathematics, penmanship, and geography. They memorized most of their lessons by reciting information over and over.

The apothecary

a mortar and pestle

The apothecary shop was located in town. Inside, its shelves were lined with bottles and jars of prepared medicines. Apothecary shops, such as the one in the picture above, had a customer area, business area, and production area where medicines were mixed.

In colonial times there were three different jobs in professional medicine. Doctors treated diseases. Surgeons treated wounds, fixed broken bones, and performed operations. Apothecaries treated illnesses, made and sold medicines, and performed surgery. Apothecaries were common because most towns weren't big enough to have doctors or surgeons. Most apothecaries trained for their job by working as apprentices.

Apothecaries made their remedies from chemicals, plants, and minerals. Most were made into liquids, but sometimes pills were made instead, because the medicine tasted bad. Some of these remedies are still being used today. For example, calamine can be used for chicken pox and poison ivy.

Taking out blood

One treatment for sickness was bloodletting. It was believed that **inflammation**—redness, swelling, heat, and pain—and some fevers were caused by improper circulation of the blood. If the blood was let out, then the symptoms would go away and the patient would get better.

A hole in the head

Most serious illnesses and accidents were treated in the patient's home. Operations could also be performed at home. One of the many operations performed in colonial times was called **trepanning**. A hole was drilled into a patient's skull if the surgeon thought pieces of bone were pressed against the brain. Because they did not know about germs in colonial times, many patients died from infections after their operations.

*Most people were bled by having a vein punctured with a knife called a **lancet**. Sometimes leeches were used to take blood from small children because their veins were too small for the lancet.*

The ladder was attached to the body of the windmill. Before the miller turned the mill, he raised the ladder. When the ladder was down, it anchored the mill to prevent it from turning.

The windmill

The windmill of Williamsburg was a gristmill. A gristmill ground grain into flour. Williamsburg's windmill was used to grind corn into cornmeal. Farmers from the surrounding areas depended on the miller for the cornmeal they used to make their bread. They would travel great distances to bring their corn to the mill because grinding corn by hand was a very difficult task. The mill operator was either a slave or was hired by the mill owner to operate the mill. The colonials paid for their cornmeal with cash or with one-sixth of the flour. Sometimes they bartered with the miller; their cornmeal was ground in exchange for farm produce, such as eggs.

Using the wind for power

The body of the windmill was placed on a pivot and supported by strong wooden posts. Because of these posts, this type of windmill was also called a **post mill**. The **tail pole**, which was connected to a wheel, allowed the miller to turn the whole mill so that it would face the wind.

The gristmill in Williamsburg used the wind as its source of power. The wind's energy turned the sails of the mill, which turned the gears. The gears then caused the top grindstone to rotate. The corn was ground between it and the bottom stone.

Working with the wind

The wind was the miller's master and servant. He often had to get up in the middle of the night to turn the windmill to face the wind. If there was no wind, the miller could not work. If the wind was too strong, it could damage the mill.

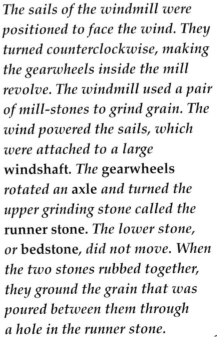

sails

windshaft

gearwheels

axle

runner stone

bedstone

The sails of the windmill were positioned to face the wind. They turned counterclockwise, making the gearwheels inside the mill revolve. The windmill used a pair of mill-stones to grind grain. The wind powered the sails, which were attached to a large **windshaft.** *The* **gearwheels** *rotated an* **axle** *and turned the upper grinding stone called the* **runner stone.** *The lower stone, or* **bedstone,** *did not move. When the two stones rubbed together, they ground the grain that was poured between them through a hole in the runner stone.*

The golden ball was the symbol commonly used by silversmiths, goldsmiths, and jewelers. In the silversmith shop above, customers could buy spoons, cups, bowls, tea strainers, and buckles for shoes.

The shops

Williamsburg had a large number of shops for its size because many people traveled there to buy things they could not purchase in their own towns. Although many products sold in the shops were made by the tradespeople in town, some shops also offered a variety of imported goods from Europe.

Tradespeople, such as this harnessmaker, were also shopkeepers. They sold their goods in the workshops where they made them.

The tradespeople

Tradespeople were skilled men and women who made goods by hand and sold them to others. They were an important part of community life. Examples of tradespeople are coopers, gunsmiths, and carpenters.

Few of the tradespeople were wealthy or well-educated. They learned their trades by working as apprentices, and made a living by selling their goods. If the goods were not well-made, people did not buy them. Tradespeople did not make a large profit on the sale of their goods because they sold their merchandise at reasonable prices.

The gunsmith made guns that were used for hunting and protection.

1

2

3

Mary Dickinson

Before you look at the caption on the opposite page, guess which shops are advertised by these signs.

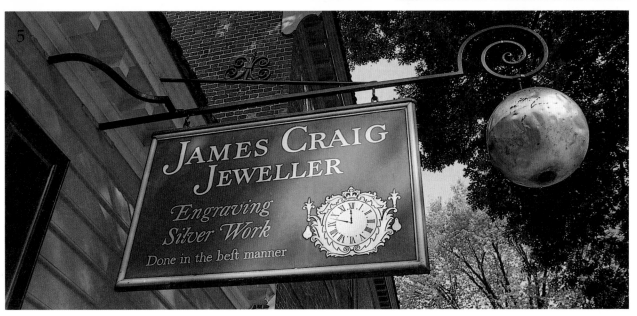

5

JAMES CRAIG
JEWELLER

Engraving
Silver Work

Done in the best manner

The sign with the pig stands for meat and other foodstuffs.

The chair on this sign indicates that furniture is made inside. It is the cabinetmaker's shop.

(Opposite page) 1. The apothecary's sign was a mortar and pestle. The mortar and pestle were used to crush medicines into powder form.
2. The sign of the wigmaker
3. Feathers and fans were special accessories available at the milliner's shop. Milliners also sold hats and articles of clothing.
4. The rhinoceros horn was believed to have great healing power. The rhinoceros was another apothecary symbol.
5. The golden ball symbolized silversmiths and goldsmiths.

Colorful signs

One cannot help but notice the colorful and imaginative signs outside the shops and taverns of Williamsburg. Each one was carefully crafted to advertise the goods or services offered by the establishment. Since some people in the eighteenth century never learned to read, many of the signs used pictures instead of words to show what was sold inside. If a person needed boots or shoes, he or she would look for a sign with a boot.

Look at the signs on these pages. Using pictures, they tell you what is sold in each shop. With a friend or a group, you can also design some picture signs that describe your home, school, or classroom. What symbols will you use?

The people of Williamsburg

The population of Williamsburg was made up of merchants, farmers, tradespeople, government officials, plantation owners, clergymen, laborers, students, and slaves. The wealthiest residents were called the **gentry**. The **middling sort** consisted of tradespeople and other shopkeepers. Most people were below these two groups. The lowest level of society consisted of black slaves who were owned for life.

(top) More than half the population of colonial Williamsburg was black. Most of these people were slaves. (bottom) Some residents of Williamsburg were very wealthy and lived in large, lovely homes.

In the early years of Virginia many people from faraway places came to live in Williamsburg. In exchange for their passage by ship they agreed to work as servants in the town. These workers were called **indentured servants**. Over time, slaves replaced indentured servants as workers.

(left) Many slaves worked in the fields, planting and harvesting tobacco and other crops.

(below) Some slaves worked as apprentices for the tradesmen in town.

Slaves from Africa

By the year 1770, about half of Williamsburg's population was made up of blacks. The tobacco plantations needed workers, so the colonials bought African slaves to do the work. Slaves had very difficult lives. They were forced to work long hours with little time off. They were separated from their families. The worst part about being a slave, however, was that slaves had few rights as human beings. They were considered someone's property.

Professionals, such as this lawyer, also lived and worked in Williamsburg. Lawyers were in demand because they represented people involved in civil law suits at the Courthouse or Capitol.

The students built models of the trade shops, trees, tools, and street lights from wood, cardboard, paper, and other available materials. The model took up most of the space in the classroom.

Project Williamsburg

A group of students learned about colonial times by turning their classroom into a replica of Colonial Williamsburg. The students researched, made plans, held discussions, solved problems, and created a masterpiece that even the colonial tradespeople would have praised!

Building a model was a little like restoring Colonial Williamsburg. Every detail had to be carefully researched and reproduced. It was hard work but a great way to learn history!

This weaving loom made by the students really worked! They learned how to weave a rug on it.

The students of Hoover Elementary School in Kenmore, New York, were proud of their colonial town. Their teacher, Art Werner, was proud of his students!

Glossary

amputation The process of cutting off a limb or part of a limb

apprentice One who is learning a trade under a skilled tradesperson

bartering The act of exchanging goods or services without the use of money

capital A town or city which houses the office of government

capitol The building in which government officials assemble to make laws

clergymen Ministers or priests who serve in a religious order

colony A territory inhabited by settlers who are governed by a distant country

community 1. A group of people who live together in one area and share buildings, services, and a way of life 2. The place in which these people live

eighteenth century The period in history ranging from the year 1701 to 1800

Historic Area The area of Williamsburg that contains restored buildings

indentured servant One who has promised services to another for a specified amount of time

milliner 1. A person skilled in designing, creating, and mending clothes 2. One who sells handmade fashion garments

muster day A gathering required by law during which militia members practiced military exercises

outbuilding A building that is separate from its main house or estate

plantation A large estate or farm on which crops are grown

produce Farm products such as grain, eggs, and vegetables

pulpit An elevated platform from which sermons are delivered in a church

rector A clergyman who is the head of a religious community

replica Something that is reproduced to look like something else

restoration The process by which something is brought back to its previous condition

settlement A small established community

slave patrol A group of militia members required by law to visit slave quarters and ensure that slaves were not gathering together or traveling illegally

statehouse A building in which a body of government conducts official business

tradespeople Workers skilled in crafts or trades

Index

apothecaries 20-21, 27
apprentices 20, 25, 29
blacks 28, 29
bloodletting 21
Bruton Parish Church 10, 18
capital 5, 7, 8, 9, 15
Capitol 10, 15, 16, 9
College of William and Mary 10, 19
colonies 5, 6, 7, 9, 16
Courthouse 10, 17, 29
Discovery, the 6
Duke of Gloucester Street 10, 12
England 5, 6, 7, 8, 14, 18, 19
explorers 6
General Assembly 16
General Court 16
Godspeed, the 6
Goodwin, Dr. W.A.R. 9
government 8, 9, 15, 16, 18, 28
governor 8, 9, 14, 15
Governor's Council 16
Governor's Palace 10, 14-15
Historic Area 4, 5, 10-11
House of Burgesses 16
indentured servants 28
inns 8, 9
James Fort 6, 7
Jamestown 6-7, 15
king of England 6, 8, 14, 15, 16, 18, 19
lawyers 29

leeches 21
Magazine 16
map of Williamsburg 10-11
Middle Plantation 8
militia 16
model of Williamsburg 30-31
outbuildings 9
pillory 17
plantations 28, 29
population 28-29
Public Gaol 10, 17
punishments 17
restoration 9
Rockefeller, John D. Jr. 9
schools 19
shopkeepers 18, 25, 28
shops 4, 9, 12, 24, 25, 26, 27, 30, 31
signs 12, 26-27
silversmiths 24, 27
slaves 17, 18, 28, 29
stocks 17, 18
students 19, 28, 30, 31
Susan Constant, the 6
taverns 8, 9, 12, 27
tobacco 7, 29
tradespeople 4, 7, 9, 24, 25, 27, 28, 29, 30
trepanning 21
Virginia 4, 5, 6, 7, 9, 15, 16, 19, 28
windmills 22-23

6 7 8 9 Printed in U.S.A. 1 0 9 8 7